THE
GOSPEL
ACCORDING TO METALLICA

KELLY MONTGOMERY

iUniverse, Inc.
Bloomington

The Gospel
According to Metallica

iUniverse books may be ordered through booksellers or by contacting:

iUniverse
1663 Liberty Drive
Bloomington, IN 47403
www.iuniverse.com
1-800-Authors (1-800-288-4677)

ISBN: 978-1-4759-3821-0 (sc)
ISBN: 978-1-4759-3822-7 (e)

Printed in the United States of America

iUniverse rev. date: 12/27/2012

CONTENTS

INTRODUCTION

The popular, and much loved comedian Jim Carrey has said, "All real change is borne out of desperation." This book was born the same way. It began as a journal, in a shed, in my back yard, in 2005. I was, at that time so drunk I could barely spell, and was pondering "the question," as presented in the first chapter. Gradually the journal morphed into this quasi-theological "treatise."

There are many valid criticisms that have been, could be, and likely, will be leveled against this quisling literary effort. The book itself stands as the only rebuttal to be offered.

The disconnected, disjointed, abrupt, non-sequential, and largely disoriented nature of the work is, if unintentional, also unapologetically presented. The reader is encouraged to "connect the dots" as needed. This is especially true of the last chapter, "Seminalia." This is just a lot of random thoughts I felt needed to be included, but that (fittingly) don't really fit in anywhere.

There are elitists, and there are egalitarians. A political

populist is more egalitarian, and tends to believe that common men matter, have a voice, and should not be lightly dismissed. An elitist, conversely, tends to think that only a select few are qualified to lead, to chose, to think, to speak. These few, they say, should be, de facto, deputized to determine what is best for everyone.

I am not an elitist. I believe the most bedrock principles of our American founders, which strangely, can in some ways be traced back to the Knights Templar (a mostly French, Christian group that evidently carried within it some powerful undercurrents of arcana), include an unshakeable devotion to the idea that the individual, the common man, has preeminent value. Without this valuation, the group (society), with the exception of the few elite, is but little more than a pack of scavenging mongrels to be managed.

Most people would agree than men have political rights. Men have rights before other men. But do men have rights before an almighty creator? Likely, the answer is no. Notwithstanding, the Christian gospel informs us that an omnipotent creator God voluntarily chose to bind himself in a covenant of service and blessing to (at least some of) his created "offspring." In pursuit of this covenant, Jesus (God's putative son) was offered in purchase and redemption of the "common man." In 1 Corinthians 2 the New Testament goes so far as to marginalize the elitist, and place him in a precarious position in regard to his potential eternal salvation… The Bible, I believe, is clearly a populist document. At least, it is at face value.

It is not my intention to attack anyone's faith. I am simply asking questions, trying hard to answer my own, and find anyone who can help shed light on some very convoluted material…

With these thoughts in mind, with offense intended toward none, and with magnanimity and love intended toward most, this common man offers you this bizarre analysis of some of the theology that may underlay some of the current popular music, its' implications, as well as certain ancient beliefs...

4 July, 2012

CHAPTER ONE
THE QUESTION

The heavy metal rock group Metallica is possibly the finest expression of art that has yet to grace the genre. Other metal groups have a gritty, grinding, chainsaw-like attack, but none of them can hold a candle to the pulsating, gut-wrenching fury that characterizes this band.

These men, James Hetfield, Kirk Hammett, Lars Ulrich, (Jason Newsted, who left the band to begin a project of his own, "Echobrain," Cliff Burton, who died in an accident in 1986, Dave Mustaine, who left the band and started a band of his own: "Megadeath") and Robert Trujillo have apparently experienced some things in life. While many mindlessly pursue their agendas for success-at-all-cost, these, at a relatively young age have grappled with some questions that most put off for the greater balance of their lives. Some never bother with them at all.

Vince Lombardi said, "Winning isn't everything, it's the

only thing." For many this is a kind of mantra. It seems to have become an American ideal. But, winning what?

When Scarlet O'hara (in Gone With the Wind) stood in a graveyard at sunset and swore to God that she would "lie, cheat, steal, or kill, but never be poor again…" it seems the American public heard that and somehow confused it for a religious credo, or statement of faith, a kind of doctrinal confession…Edmond, Oklahoma practices this faith with the utmost diligence. Houston, Texas, drives like it (reference the I-610 between 2:00 pm and 6:00!).

These Masters of Metal have done a bit better. These have dared to ask "The Question." As in The Matrix, Trinity[1] asks, "You know the question, don't you?" And Neo[2], of course, does. Only for the rest of us the question in not, "What is the matrix?" but rather, "Why are we here?"

There are only three possible answers to this question.

Answer one: We are the blind, meaningless product of an arbitrary (and cruel) evolutionary process. You have no more meaning or importance than any other highly evolved mammal, or primate. The dominance and strength you can project and sustain are the expression of, and justification for your existence. You exist for one reason, to survive, to thrive by conquest. Blind evolution has conditioned, made, molded and adapted you to compete with, manipulate, and conquer your environment. This especially includes those unfortunate, hapless, less well evolved specimens of humanity that you are reluctantly forced to consort with each day. Those lost, stupid, slow-minded, brutish, lazy,

---

1   Played by Carrie Ann Moss
2   Played by Keanua Reeves

undereducated rabble that have not reached the exalted pinnacle of evolutionary sophistication that you enjoy. It is your job to bring order to this chaos of human folly, and to rule it well. This is your birthright as the superior being that you are. You must conquer, or be conquered. You are just an advanced animal, and it is only natural that you act like one. God has nothing to do with it.

Answer two: We were created by an almighty, omnipotent personage who meticulously designed and crafted every aspect of creation and your being with a lazer-like specificity of purpose.

Answer three: Some compromise between the first two views.

CHAPTER TWO
THE GODS

For example, there are many gods, none being supreme. This is called polytheism, and if one rejects the Bible as revelation, it is easily the oldest and the original belief system. All other beliefs would have to have sprung from this origin. If, conversely, God created Adam, he would have inculcated within him an understanding of himself, and his nature, which Adam would have transmitted to his progeny. Quickly, however, in history this belief would prove unpopular, no doubt because of its' innately restrictive nature, and its' emphasis on personal responsibility to a Creator. These two would naturally be antithetical to one another, and mutually intolerant for obvious reasons.

The great counterpart to polytheism is pantheism. This is the belief that God is not only everywhere and in everything, he actually is everything, and everything is him. A well known modern proponent of this idea is the actress, dancer, and bestselling author Shirley MacLain. She is famous for standing on the beach and saying, "I am God, I am God..."

Henry Morris is a great champion of the scientific creationist point of view. He astutely observes that all polytheistic belief systems are inherently evolutionary. In his book Education for the Real World, he states on pages 55 and following:

> "Darwinism is not new at all but merely a revival of pagan philosophy"... the Greek philosophers propounded an idea "very similar, if not quite identical, to modern evolutionary cosmogonies. Very similar constructs will be found in the writings of ancient Chinese and Hindu philosophies, as well as those of Egypt, Assyria, and other ancient nations. Such evolutionary ideas of cosmogony universally coincided with pantheistic concepts of cosmology. The cosmos itself was the ultimate reality. God and nature were synonymous. Though the great World Spirit was everywhere, this pantheistic god could be locally worshipped as the god of the river, goddess of the forest, etc. Thus a great pantheon of gods and goddesses emerged, all actually mere personifications of the various forces and systems of nature. This pantheon was essentially the same in all ancient nations, though different names were given to individual deities in different nations and languages. Further, all were associated with two other systems, spiritism (or animism) and astrology."

The point being that, God is nature, and that he himself is evolving. His beginning, as that of the universe at large is uncertain, but what is known is that everything is evolving upward, including humans. Though most modern physicists acknowledge and accept the "Big Bang" theory of origins, few attempt to take the next step backward and explain what, if anything caused the bang. Fewer still are willing to acknowledge the inherent contradiction between the known fact that everything in the universe is subject to the laws of entropy (or deterioration), and how it could be evolving upward at the same time...

Animism is the belief in and worship of nature spirits, the belief that spirits (gods) reside in mountains, rocks, trees, rivers, and so on. Shamanism is an offshoot of this. A shaman is an individual who has special contact and sensitivity to the spirit world, and serves as a link or bridge to if for the common person.

A well known modern exposition of the concept of pantheism is to be found in the Star Wars movies, as when Obie Wan deftly explains the "force" that empowers and guides the Jedi.

Virtually all the great civilizations and cultures from the remotest antiquity were an amalgam of poly and pantheism. The cultures of Babylon, Assyria, Egypt, China, Persia, and later those "across the pond" in North and South America, the Inca, Maya, Aztec, Olmec, Toltec, and American Indian tribes all followed the same pattern of settling down near a major river, irrigating, and worshipping a remarkably similar panoply of gods.

The distinction between polytheism and pantheism is most importantly a difference between an impersonal "force," and gods that are more human. These gods have names, and personalities that humans can identify with, and relate to.

Modern Hinduism is an excellent representative of this

category of belief. It contains elements of both polytheism and pantheism. It has many personal gods such as Krishna, Ganesh, and Kali. It also carries the idea of an impersonal force, such as Karma, and Brahmin.

Shintoism, the beliefs of the American Indians, and of cultures found throughout the modern world all reflect animism and shamanism in our modern world.

CHAPTER THREE
THE ONE GOD

Polytheism and pantheism are the middle ground between the two more stark options of belief. One of these is atheism. If there is no God, then everything had to have evolved. How do you know? We are here aren't we? Some of the more brilliant modern philosophers even question that!

The trend today, even in the most avant-garde scientific schools of thought is to lean toward some kind of Intelligent Design theory. If one rejects the traditional religions, this invariably leads one to accept some form of New Age credo or other.

Assuming that we are not the figments of our own imaginations, and if we bypass poly and pan, we are left with atheism and its' opposite: monotheism. There are four major monotheistic belief systems in the world, and they are the only four of any consequence. They are well known, and three of the four are still widely followed. The fourth, Zoroastrianism was a dynamic force in ancient Persian culture.

This faith was founded by Zoroaster, also known as Zarathustra. He was the prophet of the Supreme Being known as Ahura-Mazda. The practice of this system has all but died out in the modern world. Of the few surviving remnants of it are a group in Mumbai (formerly "Bombay"), India, "being a small and highly westernized community of less than 100,000 souls…" according to R. C. Zaehner, author of a definitive work on the subject called, "The Dawn and Twilight of Zoroastrianism." These are called the Parsees, and are direct descendants of their Persian/Iranian forbears. The faith they practice is a modified, modernized version of the ancient system. There is a "new" and thriving system of thought based upon the counterpart of Ormazd (his other name), Ahriman, the other creative spirit in the universe, who is the nemesis and combatant to Ahura, and presents a legitimate challenge to him… Ahriman is a spirit of chaos and destruction. This faith is called, naturally, "The Church of Ahriman."

In Iran itself, approximately 10,000 Zoroastrians live in villages called Yazd, and Kerman. Their faith has elements of monotheistic belief, as well as occult overtones. In addition, there are a few remaining fire-temples which have survived from antiquity, and are tolerated by the strongly Shi'ite Islamic regime there.

Islam is founded on a belief in the Supreme Being known as Allah. Many equate Allah with God, but the beliefs and practices associated with the two are starkly different. If they are one and the same, then this deity appears to be suffering from an acute form of associative identity (multiple personality) disorder. Islam does accept and subsume many of the beliefs and assumptions found in its' two predecessors.

These two predecessors are of course Judaism, and Christianity, which grew out of it. They both accept and believe the Old Testament of the Bible. The New Testament is rejected by the Jews, as is the entire belief system of Christianity. Many Jews regard Jesus not as the Christ (Messiah), but as an imposter who was properly crucified for firing up a false new spin of the Old Testament revelation. His followers are charged with intentionally conjuring up the myth of his resurrection from the dead, for which this faith is so well known.

Another serious breach between these two is the universal Christian teaching of the Trinity, that God is actually three persons in one. Many Jews and Muslims reject this idea as absurd, and maintain that Christians actually worship three gods, not the one, true God.

An in depth comparison of Christianity and its' two monotheistic counterparts is not within the scope or intention of this book.

This leaves us with what we will call the "three colors" of Christian-based monotheism: Grey, White, and Black. Grey monotheism would be the belief that there is one God who created everything, and that he is morally "neutral." This could be characterized by the teaching known as Deism. A famous holder of this opinion was the founding father, Thomas Jefferson. This belief says that God created the world, then took an extended leave of absence, and has not returned since. He does not interact with his creation at all, and never will.

There are some problems with this point of view. First, God could not be morally neutral if he went off and left his creation to itself. This would be like the proverbial "baby on the doorstep." To completely shrug off any responsibility for the world, and do absolutely nothing to help is hardly a stance to be placed in the category of neutrality. Further, where would he go? How could he not see, hear, and know what was going on here, if he is truly omniscient? And if he is omnipresent, how could he not be present here in some sense?

Another version of "Grey monotheism" is something that many modernist denominations teach de facto. They present God as an inept, bumbling fool. He would like to help more, but he just can't. He doesn't seem to have the power to. Or, he is just stupid. He just doesn't quite seem to "get it." He isn't entirely aware of what is happening, or he would be glad to help. They never come out and say these things, but their teaching and praying often leaves this distinct impression.

Yet another form of Grey monotheism would be that found in the Zoroastrian model. In it, God (called Ahura –Mazda) is in a serious competition with his adversary, Ahriman (this is the Persian name of a personage who generally corresponds to the western concept of "the Devil," yet goes much farther. The more familiar name "Satan" means adversary, and is of Hebrew origin). Ahura is in a bitter life and death struggle to defeat this bright, formidable upstart spirit that also has the power to create, and threatens to hijack the universe. This UFC-like, cosmic cagefight is for the highest of all purses, but its' outcome is far from uncertain. In Zarathustra's eschatological prognostication, good wins decisively over evil (by TKO, as it were) and "the lie." However, here again, what if Mr. Zoro got it wrong? What if the Ahrimanists are right, and this fight is still open, as to outcome?

It may be possible that God could be characterized by Grey monotheism, but if this is true it is bluntly contradictory to the clearly enunciated portrait found in the Old Testament, and echoed in the New.

Next, you have "White Monotheism." This is the classic, standard concept of God, as most of us (here in the U.S.) have been brought up with. In this system God is the glorious ruler of the universe. He is righteous and perfectly holy. He is good, and infinitely powerful. He knows everything, loves his creation, and would never abandon it, even for a second. Everything he does is virtuous and benevolent, in both intent, and outcome.

The big problem with this is obvious. If God is so good, why is his creation so screwed up? Any Creator who would allow his creation to totter and spin so precariously, has some real issues! To allow death in the first place is bad enough, but such death! There is death on a mass scale, death of infants, children, young adults with families. There is death by disease, by violence, warfare, and accidents. There is genocide, patricide, infanticide, suicide, and graveside. It goes on and on… No deity who is at the helm of reality and knowingly, willingly allows all this without some astonishingly ameliorating purpose for it all can possibly be good. One might almost be tempted to re-lyric the famous Newton hymn:

> "Amazing death, how dark the sound!
> That slaughters fools like me;
> I looked around and carnage found,
> And blood on all I see!"

There is suffering, misery, poverty, puberty, torture, murder, mayhem and drowning. There is SIDS, AIDS, KIDS, and—you get the point. And since the notion of a good, holy, loving, merciful, compassionate God has been given a fairly sufficient amount of press already, let's consider for a moment the alternative possibility.

And that is what we will call "Black Monotheism." This is what Metallica is setting forth to their listeners. In this, God is everything he is thought to be in all the other monotheistic viewpoints, with this notable exception: he is inherently evil. He just doesn't care about human suffering. To the contrary, he gets off on it. In fact, that is basically why he made the world—so he could have something to laugh at! Sort of like when a mean kid sets fire to the dog, or throws a cat off the roof of a building, just for kicks.

But what if Metallica is right? Is that really a possibility? What if God is really not good? First, let's establish what probably everyone would agree with, that there is at least some good in the world. The world, creation, nature is not, cannot be entirely evil.

Look at creation, or nature. There are some beautiful things out there. There are stars, forests, the sky, the ocean and the beach, sunlight, flowers, babies, women, steaks, oranges, '65 GTO's, rainbows, real blueberry pies (though these are rare), kangaroos, ducks, colors, especially orange, beer, laughter, etc. Never mind that nearly all these things under certain conditions can and will kill you. The world has beauty. No one denies this. So, if God is evil, why would he bother to create (or allow) beauty?

In the climax of the third Star Wars movie, Obie Wan and Annikin are battling on a lava planet. It is a place of intense heat, fire, and constant volcanic upheaval. Earth could have been created to be like that. It could be an infernal, never-ending state of pain, grief and strife. There are those who would say that life on Earth is like that: a constant state of lethal competition for supremacy, and a world of continuous suffering and torment. But is our world really that bad? Is life here on this Earth a continual state of unrelenting suffering and agony? Hardly. Though people may often say that hell is here on Earth, I think most of us would poo-poo such an idea. Even the most cynical and pessimistic among us would have to admit that there are good times, fun, pleasure, and yes, even moments of joy and ecstasy.

As in The Lord of the Rings, Sam Gamgee so poignantly observes, "There is good in this world, Mr. Frodo, and it's worth fighting for!" And if there is good here in this life, it is hard to square with the idea that God is evil. Why would an evil Supreme Being be troubled with the existence of good? Why would he not carefully sift out all trace of goodness or happiness from this life, and ensure that it could never enter into the picture at all?

Is God unable to completely eradicate all the good, happiness, laughter, hope, peace and love that exists? Or is the appearance of good only an illusion? Is it just a cover, a façade, a fake front to trick us so we will keep trying to climb to the top of this ever-imploding heap of cosmic putrefaction, this black hole of meanness?

Is this world just a backdrop for the true and underlying secret purpose of "blinding, twisting, smashing and laughing," that God is really up to? Is the good we think we see and feel a huge mirage, an immense delusion? Is this clever, malicious puppet master merely practicing, "Tuwi asoni man…" (fattening up the pig for the slaughter: a reference to the practice of cannibals who befriend and deceive the poor victim of their next culinary aspiration, as depicted in the gripping missionary account called Lords of the Earth by Don Richardson) on our dark, deceived, fevered minds?

Perhaps, if He didn't give us at least some happiness we would, lemming-like, commit a concerted mass suicide and collectively end our existence on the planet. (The Greens might enjoy this one! Then the animals would have it all to themselves...arf, arf...).

It is a common practice among Christians to pray before they consume food, to thank God for giving it to them. In scripture, Christ boasts of His Father's great magnanimity by sending rain and sunshine on the unjust and evil, as well as upon the good. But is this really valid?

If God did not feed anyone, soon there would be no one alive. Who then would be left to sing "Amazing Grace" next Sunday morning? As Moses said, "the Egyptians will hear..." The universe would know that this merciful God, is maybe not so merciful. How could God sift and strain out sunshine and rain from the unworthy, and grant it only to the "good?" Or is this perhaps what hell is? Is it a concentration camp of torment for the bad, where every possible drop of hope, comfort, and rest has been eternally drained and strained away and removed? Even so, here and now rain and sunshine are necessary to sustain life on the Earth. For God to withhold these would presage annihilation for the entire race.

Does God hold any moral obligation whatever to His creation? Or, as Deism opines, is he free to create, and then utterly abandon? Would that qualify Him to carry the title "merciful?" Where is the mercy in that?

CHAPTER FOUR
THE BIG THREE

Or, Enter John Calvin

John Calvin was in some ways one of the most seminal men in history. No, he did not sire a huge number of children, but he did make a big dent in thinking. He articulated the idea that one's personal salvation, as well as the larger picture of world history, including fate, destiny (or whatever name or term one prefers) and the future has already been determined. This determination is irrevocably dictated in what theologians call "the decrees of God." The idea was not original with Mr. Calvin, but was largely ignored until he popularized it.

This teaching (which has always somehow carried a disproportionate blast of energy with it), along with the translation and dissemination of the Bible (for the first time in history) to the common man, aided by the invention of the printing press, were factors largely responsible for fueling the

Protestant Reformation. This came at a time when the world was turning the corner from Middle to Modern age, and was open to new ways of looking at everything, including God.

The Protestant Reformation in turn was largely responsible for both sparking and fueling the scientific basis for the modern era (please see Alister McGrath's comprehensive coverage of this in his excellent book, "Christianity's Dangerous Idea"). In many places, the Bible does clearly say that God not only controls the outcome of events, but that He "foreknew" and "elected" to render them in a certain way. There is no "random," no luck, no "fate" as we usually conceive it.

Every event, large and small, even down to the death of sparrows and the loss of hair on one's head (including the remaining number) is carefully calculated, counted, and controlled (Matt. 10:30). Its' disposal and outcome were decided and settled in what is often called "eternity past" (the period before creation, before time or matter existed, before Gen 1:1).

The decision, agreement and determination that Jesus Christ would be "slain from (before) the foundation of the world" was made during this "pre-time" period.

In this view, God's entire plan and purpose in creation is founded, based and centered upon that number known as "the elect" or "chosen." These chosen are like the picture, and creation is merely the frame. They are the jewel, the world only the setting. They are the flowers of the garden, all else only the soil.

In fact, the entire universe is a massive backdrop created specifically to provide a stage upon which the "drama of redemption" may play out: that colossal and sweeping enactment that culminates in the Cross, the 2nd coming of Christ, and the

Resurrection. In Biblical terms, this is often likened to many things, but notable among these analogies it the comparison to a military conquest. Salvation is "the victory," and Christ's return is clearly inbued with a martial significance. He is coming to "conquer" and to "defeat" his "enemies."

And who are His enemies? Anyone not numbered among his "elect." These are the "saved," the "saints," and "when they go marchin' in," it will be at the climax of history when they victoriously received the "Kingdom," prepared and purchased for them by Christ, the King. This is the one you are talking about when you pray, "Thy kingdom come…"

In Biblical parlance there is only one universe. It has only one God, who had only one son who died only one time, in one place, on one planet, for one people. There are no aliens, no multiplicity of inhabited planets, no other worlds.

There are only men, angels, and devils, and the focus and locus of all three is right here on good old planet Earth.

The whole point and purpose of reality is to please and glorify God as he orchestrates a cosmic chess match, a love story, and overwhelming invasion, and on and on…

In the end, because of guts, grace, gray matter and goodness, God gets the girl, the gold, and the gun…(!) He wins it all to the shame, ruin, destruction, and everlasting infamy of all who opposed Him, and refused to accept, submit to, and believe him. These may be construed as God's enemies.

However, there is a big hitch. If, as many gospel preachers maintain, all men are able to simply accept or reject this message, then all is well. But a careful fidelity to Calvinist theology precludes this. If man can chose God, or chose not to love or obey Him, then there is a level playing field. Everyone has an equal chance, and Jesus is "an equal opportunity Savior." God is fair, and "all's right with the world." This is not, unfortunately, what Mr. Calvin (and the Bible) said.

It is not, in the final analysis man that chooses God. It is God that does the choosing. He initiates (Heb 12:1-2), conforms the will (Phil 2:13-14), and changes the very nature of the sinner to that of saint (Eph 2).

The biblical analogies of this change are numerous and multifarious. Christians are changed from goats to sheep, lost to found, blind to sighted, servant to friend, briar to grapevine, weed to wheat, leper to cleansed, dead to living, child of darkness to child of light, alien to citizen, fool to wise, stained to clean, wounded, bruised and pestilent to healed and healthy, usurping squatter to rightful heir, poor to wealthy, slave to son, morally unclean to holy, contaminated and filthy to pure, and the list could be extended indefinitely.

Perhaps the most striking and germane aspect of these comparisons is that the basis for them all is the simple declarative proclamation that they become true because, and at the moment God says so. This event is a unique act, individual to each and every believer. It is as when God spoke in creation and the mere articulation of the words caused them to become a reality (2 Corinthians 4:6-7). And though the various branches of Christianity see and describe the specifics of this event differently, the result is always the same: a person believes, and a life is changed.

As in the creation, so here (2 Cor 4:6-7), the sinner is transformed from present status to "new creation" by the sheer force of God's intention that it be so. The vehicle by which this change is enacted and accomplished is faith. This faith itself is caused, given, granted and engaged by the purpose, word, and will of God. It was intended, allowed for, planned, purposed, and caused by God. The sinner is merely the recipient and beneficiary of the change. God is the giver, man is the getter...

There is no pre-condition, hence, it is called "unconditional election" (the U in the famous Calvinist acrostic, TULIP). There is no preparation or endeavor which can pre-qualify one, or even increase the chances of the being among the chosen.

People are chosen of "Every race, language, nation," and status. In fact, wealth, intelligence, education (Mat 10, 1 Cor 2), and beauty, all the qualities most admired by this world, are, if anything, more likely to cause one to be passed over (Luke 16-the rich man).

The Holy Spirit alone (the 3rd person of the Trinity) energizes the recipient of God's merciful choice to respond to his initiatory overtures. "We love him because he first loved..." (1 John 4:19). Only God knows who the elect are, or will be.

This brings up a thorny point of disagreement among many Christians. The Arminian Protestant position, as well as the Roman Catholic is much softer on the Divine initiation of a sinner's interest in salvation. Calvin would say that no one, absolutely no one would ever show any interest in God's offer of salvation if God himself did not initiate the process, then follow through with it. Consequently, no one, not one human, would ever be saved. Heaven would be empty, like a ghost town, except for the original inhabitants: the angels, and God.

Here is the "T" in the famous Calvinist "TULIP," total

depravity. This does not say that man has no good in him, but that no part of man is free of the taint and contamination of sin. Therefore man's reason, and moral faculties, since the fall are so vitiated that no one would ever be able to muster enough interest or desire for God to respond to the offer of the gospel. That is, unless God enabled them to. This teaching is called "inability" ("No man can come unto me...John 5, 6, etc.).

The Catholics would not entirely agree. They contend that all men have a choice. They also say God must initiate grace, but then and at that point man is enabled to co-operate with this grace and do things to make himself more compatible with God's working. It is as if God clears the ground and fertilizes and waters it. He agrees to provide sunshine. He provides the seeds and one might even say plants the first few. After that it is up to man to carefully take over the job and cultivate the ground and be sure that it produces. God assists, but man has an integral responsibility to help it be productive. If he does a good job he is rewarded with more seed, sunshine, etc. If he screws it up, then God patiently tries again and again if need be, to re-initiate the whole process.

In fact, the Catholic system is in most respects by far the most merciful of the three major systems of salvific theology, as I call them, the Big Three. They are: 1. Catholic Arminian, 2. Protestant Arminian, and 3. Protestant Calvinist. [There was once a movement within the Catholic Church that embraced elective theology known as Jansenism. It was condemned as a heresy starting in 1640 through a series of Papal Bulls. It was somewhat of a reactionary teaching to offset the Protestant Reformers teachings through such notables as Beza, Luther, and

Calvin. It was stridently opposed by the Jesuits, who, in the end won out and sanitized the Catholic Church of the hated doctrine. Had this not happened, historically, the Protestant/Catholic split would have resulted in two churches without a fig's worth of difference in their teachings, in regard to elective theology.] No one in the Christian faith will ever see heaven without entering through one of these three doors. Yet, I believe they are all the same door, seen and understood somewhat differently... (Jesus said, "I am the door... " John 10:14).

The term Arminian refers to the teachings of one Jacob Arminius who, in turn, based his ideas largely on a fourth century theologian named Pelagius. Pelagius was a contemporary (and opponent) of the redoubtable Augustine of Hippo (Hippo was a city of Carthage, North African colony of Rome.) In his view, it would be silly and unjust for God to demand repentance of people who were incapable of it. Therefore, he elevated the freewill of man to becoming the most important aspect of salvation. Without man's will being activated, no deal.

In the Catholic system, God's desire is to save all men, and Jesus provisionally died for, and redeemed all men. It is a kind of potential redemption that is paid for, but must be personally accessed to do one any good. You might compare it to money deposited in an account that is available, but must be accessed to do one any good. This access, of course, is through the sacraments of the Church. Each man's personal salvation is based on his own free will choice, and response. God's pursuit of sinners does not even end with the grave. God still allows for a person to be salvaged after death by means of the purifying fires of purgatory.

The Catholics also introduce a word that Protestants patently reject: merit. They say that man can and does (by God's grace and with his help) merit more grace, and that he eventually acquires righteousness. He actually becomes good, and the more good he becomes, the more grace he merits, and so on until he becomes saintly – and in some cases is actually inducted into that rarified number who are formally declared by the church to be saints...

Protestant Arminianism is similar to this. It also allows for human free will. The main difference is on the issue of merit. Protestants deny that there is such a thing. We have none, nor can we ever, by any means whatever, gain any. In this system, (and in this they hold with the Calvinists) salvation is completely by God's grace, and as the Lutherans like to quote their namesake: "Salvation is by grace, through faith, plus nothing." Grace plus nothing. So, after years of "godly living," the saved sinner is just as "filthy, defiled, and bankrupt" as he was the day he believed. He is only declared to be righteous by God's imputation.

Imputation is a little used, but important theological term. It is also translated, "counted," or "reckoned." Paul in his Epistle to the Romans, in chapters 4 and 5 uses this word some seven times. It is impossible to adequately explain the New Testament concept of salvation without it. It is a forensic (legal) word that carries something of the idea of a judge in a courtroom, or a king or governor issuing a formal pardon to a known criminal. He is declared not only to be not guilty, but righteous (this is something no human judge or king can do). This is done on the basis of the atonement of Christ. The sinner not only is granted a complete pardon and exoneration of all guilt, past, present, and future, but is also given the status of the very righteousness of Christ himself. This is done by the simple, declarative act of God. God speaks pardon and renewal, and it is legally done in the courtroom of heaven. This pardon is irrevocable, and immutable. There is no more penalty; there is only favor. All the sinner has to do to receive this amazing bargain is to believe and accept it. That's it! This acceptance is done by faith. This is where the Catholics have a problem. They complain that in this schema, the "rotting, putrefying leprosy of sin" remains intact and untreated, while the sinner is merely covered by a beautiful garment (salvation: Christ's righteousness) to hide the corruption below. They say that what is needed is actual righteousness, through merit, which is gained by adherence to the sacerdotal system.

Contrary to the Catholic way, the Protestants say that if a sinner dies "outside of Christ" he has absolutely no hope. There is no more mercy, no purgatory, and no second chance. There is only an eternity of fiery torment to expect. In this view, as well as in Calvinism, most of the human race from Adam and on has eternally perished in hell, and this grim prognosis continues today.

Strangely, in this view, God does love everyone, and wants all men to be saved. Jesus died for all men, but what stands in the way of the salvation of the human race is the free will of man. God would like to save all men, but is thwarted by man's adamant refusal. Here also the salvation of mankind is mostly dependent upon – mankind. Men must agree to take the gospel, and when it arrives, men must agree to accept the gospel, or it's no deal. God is largely sidelined. He is allowed to assist in the process from time to time, but he never interferes. This elevates the freewill of man to an almost sovereign level, and this is where the Calvinists step in, and take this whole issue to the next level.

The Calvinist model is by far the most stark and austere. In it, God has already chosen his elect (the word "elect" means "choice," or chosen) from the "foundation of the world" (Revelation 17:8, 1 Peter 1:20 etc.). This means before the world even existed, God had already chosen who would be saved. Here God is 100% responsible for man's response. Without his "prevenient, enabling" grace, imputation of righteousness, and maintenance of the sinner in a state of grace, absolutely no one would be saved. In addition, Jesus died specifically for the elect, and for them alone. This constitutes the "L" in TULIP, and stands for "limited atonement." It is largely rejected by most modern Protestants and Catholics, for obvious reasons. Since God is the one who must bring all this about, without man's help, he has a 100% batting average. Like a cruise missile that always hits its' target, he Mountie-like "always gets his man." This is known as "irresistible grace," and is the "I" in TULIP. Actually, man may resist for a time (reference the whale swallowed prophet, Jonah, or the former Christian killing Pharisee turned apostle, Paul), but like the Johnstown, Pennsylvania dam, his resistance is eventually flushed away and he cooperates, collaborates, and surrenders to God's call of salvation. To "surrender to Christ" is a commonly used gospel metaphor… His very *will* is changed ("for it is God that worketh in you both to will and to do of his good pleasure…" Philippians 2:13).

It is as if God has planted a "mole" within the will of his elect, and they, in spite of themselves, become "unwillingly willing" to obey him. You may ask any Christian you know about this, and they will all pretty much tell you the same thing, only in their own words. Even they themselves cannot entirely account for, or explain it. As Charles Spurgeon, the great English preacher of the 19th century liked to quote John Erskine, "I came with full consent against my will…"

But, in such a view, does God love all men? What about those he does *not* chose? Even the Puritans, those Bible-savy masters of exegesis differed on this thorny issue. It seems self-contradictory to say that God loves all men, but only bothers to save some. Some Calvinists assert that this is not so. They say that God hated some from eternity. They do have scripture to support this. Malachi 1:2-3 says, "I have loved you, saith the LORD. Yet ye say, Wherein hast thou loved us? (a common question even today!) Was not Esau Jacob's brother? Saith the LORD: yet I loved Jacob, and I hated Esau…" This is quoted by Paul in his objection swatting polemic found in chapter 9 of Romans, where he answers those who question this austere teaching. The idea that God not only elects his people to heaven, but chooses the rest for hell is called double predestination, and is the most hard line stance of all Calvinists, but held by relatively few. In fact, it is about the hardest line ever claimed by anyone to be taken by God, with the possible exception of some Muslims.

Perhaps the best handling of this is by the popular modern theologian and preacher, John MacArthur. In his excellent book, *The God Who Loves*, he explains that it is in the good, benevolent nature of God to love all his creation, but that he has a special, effectual, saving love only for his beloved elect. This love is quite indomitable (and why should it not be if God is omnipotent?).

As with a chain, there is both overlap, and connection between the three systems. If each, individual tenet of the three views is compared to one link, they share many links. However, each also has links not shared by the other two. The result is one chain. Yet, in spite of the stark, often violent historical differences (even wars that have been fought), there are no inherent or critically vital doctrinal contradictions in any of the three systems, so as to render them mutually incompatible! As in the story of the three blind men confronted with an elephant for the first time, each describes, accurately, his own perception. Yet not until the three are combined does the true picture emerge. This opinion is grossly unpopular, yet I believe it to be true, nonetheless...

The breakpoint, or cutoff between Calvinism/Arminianism is freewill vs. election. The breakpoint between Catholic and Protestant is infusion vs. imputation, or merit vs. mercy. To sum up, Calvinists say: "God chooses, God saves, Period." Arminians: "You choose, but God saves" (never mind that God also influences, and initiates this choosing). Catholics: "You choose (after God initiates, and makes possible, which goes right back to what Calvin said), then you are permitted to participate as God and you cooperate to do the saving..." Many Protestants would scoff at this idea of cooperation, but if someone was pulling you off the side of a mountain, would you not assist by tying the rope around your waist? Apparently, in Calvin's model, you are unconscious...

As to the question of *why* God loves some, and not others in this special way, no one even tries to answer. To do so would be purest speculation, because the Bible is silent on the matter.

About the closest it ever comes to an answer is in Deuteronomy 7:8 where it simply says, "because the LORD loved you…" which, obviously begs the question, "*Why* did God love me, and not my neighbor, Joe?" The answer is bound up in the mind and heart of God. There are two reasons given. For God's own pleasure, and for his own glory (Rev. 4:11, and Isaiah 43:7).

Though the Bible does often use inclusive, universalist language, it also uses limiting language in reference to the intention and scope of the gospel. It says God would have "all men to be saved, and to come to the knowledge of the truth" (1 Timothy 2:1), "not willing that *any* should perish, but that all should come to repentance" (2 Peter 3:9), "the grace of God that bringeth salvation hath appeared to all men…" (Titus 2:13). Then there is what is perhaps the most famous and oft quoted verse in all the Bible, the ubiquitous John 3:16, "For God so loved the world that he gave his only begotten son, that whosoever believeth in him should not perish, but have everlasting life…"

Conversely, there are other passages which run the other way, such as, "many be called, but few chosen…" (Matthew 20:16), "No man can come to me except the father which hath sent me draw him…" (John 6:44), or one of the most definitive on the subject, Romans 9:11-18, "For the children being not yet born, neither having done any good or evil, that the purpose of God according to election might stand, not of works, but of him that calleth; As it is written, Jacob have I loved, but Esau have I hated. What shall we say then? Is there unrighteousness with God? God forbid. For he saith to Moses, I will have mercy on whom I will have mercy, and I will have compassion on whom I will have compassion. So then it is not of him that willeth, nor of him that runneth, but of God that showeth mercy. Therefore he hath mercy on whom he will have mercy, and whom he will, he hardeneth..."

Just as in the great controversy regarding the deity of Christ, which was debated until the fourth century, so here, the Bible is teaching two mutually contradictory, incompatible concepts. As with that, that Jesus was simultaneously God, and man. Here, that man is responsible, and has free will (to some extent), yet that God has already chosen. It simply cannot logically be both ways. Yet it is.

To get back to our initial question, have the musicians of Metallica slandered a loving, merciful God? If all men truly are included in the gospel offer and in effect exclude themselves by stubborn refusal to respond, then God is not to blame. The remedy is out there, but man refuses to acknowledge, or accept it. He, like Melville's Ahab in Moby Dick, prefers to pursue his selfish, insane obsession into the dark depths of eternity... But, if the Calvinists are right, the poor, brutalized slave puppet depicted by Metallica has absolutely no chance to be saved, and never did have any...

Is God really in the business of "blinding and twisting minds, smashing dreams, and pulling men's strings" to their destruction? Does the Bible even hint at such an aspect of the character of God? Perhaps it does...

CHAPTER FIVE
THE GUN

Or "Does God Deceive People?"

At first glance the question seems absurd. Doesn't the Bible say in Titus 1:2, "God that cannot lie?" Or in James 1:13, "God cannot be tempted with evil, neither tempteth he any man." Then in Deuteronomy 32:4, "He is the rock, his work is perfect for all his ways are judgement (justice), a God of truth, and without iniquity, just and right is he..."

But what does the Bible also say?

Jeremiah, the famous "weeping prophet," accuses God of intentional, direct deception in his book, chapter 20, verse 7 where he says, "O LORD, thou hast deceived me, and I was deceived: thou art stronger than I, and hast prevailed: I am in derision daily, everyone mocketh me." The Catholic Bible uses the stronger word, "deluded." The picture is that Jeremiah is called and commissioned by God to go and warn the inhabitants of Jerusalem and Judea of the immanent invasion by the Babylonian army. He is under the impression that if he goes to preach, the people will, like Ninevah, Assyria, repent, and God will relent from the intended destruction. This, however, is not what happens. The people do not believe him, nor do they give up their cherished worship of idols. The destruction is right on schedule, and even worse. Now that the people have been warned, and have ignored the warning, their fate is sealed. Not only that, but they think that Jeremiah is a traitor who has sold out to Israel's enemies!

Poor Jeremiah is stuck in the middle. He is hated by his own people, tricked by God, and now he begins to loath his own existence, as a miscreant fool. He curses the very day of his birth! (Job also did this, in the throes of his trial.) Now we know why he is called the weeping prophet! And sure enough the predicted event did take place in a triad of invasions culminating in 586 B.C. when Jerusalem was sacked, and the temple (Solomon's renowned edifice) was completely destroyed by the Babylonian army. Jeremiah describes these events in his book of (what else?) Lamentations. The language there is both heart rending, and graphic.

This is not the only place where the Bible indicates that God deceives people. In an obscure (and rarely discussed) account found in 1 Kings 22, a little known prophet named Micaiah states that God personally, directly dispatched a "lying spirit," (who volunteers for the job!) to go forth and deceive King Ahab into pursuing his futile intention of doing battle with Syria. This results in the defeat of Israel, and the bizarre death of

Ahab himself. Here again, God deceives, then destroys. Sadly, the scope of the deception gets worse!

In the New Testament book of 2 Thessalonians 2:11 we read, "and for this cause God shall send them strong delusion, that they should believe a lie..." The "them" are all the people who live on the earth, with the exception of the elect. The delusion being referred to is the well-known and dreaded anti-christ who many believe is soon to appear. The prediction is repeated in Revelation 13:8, "and all that dwell upon the earth shall worship him," and again in Luke 21:34-35, "and take heed to yourselves [lest] that day come upon you unawares. For as a snare (a net or trap) shall it come upon all them that dwell on the face of the whole earth."

So, God is not only willing to deceive one man, or one nation to its' own destruction, but the entire world! And who is the active agent involved in this deception? Why, who else but Satan? He is well known for this. But at times the Bible clearly uses language that seems to show that God and Satan form a sort of temporary partnership for the purpose of deception. Yikes! Does this not begin to sound like Ozzy Osboune's Iron Man, who "kills the people he once saved?"

Perhaps the musicians of Metallica have, after all, a legitimate complaint.

"Your honor, what we have here is a smoking gun......"

CHAPTER SIX
THE WIZARD

Or, "The Wicked Wizard of the West "

If God deceives the people he wants to destroy; if God chooses people before they are ever born; if God not only allows, but enables and cooperates with Satan to enslave and tyrannize poor, captured victims of delusion, then how can he be truly good?

No matter how much good press or religious/Christian spin God may receive (or create), can we truly and objectively know his nature? Don't we already "have it in writing" that he may not be the "blessed Redeemer" we were told to expect? If he isn't truly good, why would he drop the dime on himself and allow us, Dorothy-like, to peer behind the curtain of mystery and see his real self revealed, only to discover a dark side?

All monotheistic belief systems agree that if God did not reveal aspects of himself to humanity, it would be impossible to know anything about his nature. Psalm 19 indicates (as well as

Romans 1-2) that God reveals himself by three primary means: creation (nature), the written word (Bible), and the internal conscience and spiritual awareness that human beings (and only humans) have (ever seen a dog pray?).

The Ten Commandments preceded Moses. All he did was to record them. Otherwise Cain could not have been held culpable for the murder of his little brother, Abel (an encouraging beginning for the first human out of the batch…). Even the most primitive cultures have intrinsic beliefs that prohibit murder, incest, and theft. Common sense alone supports the basic ideas contained in the decalouge. If there is a Creator, it stands to reason that he would give his Creation some basic instructions, an owner's manual. Societies would (and some do) quickly implode in the absence of a basic moral code.

All major cultures and civilizations throughout history that have reached any height of progress at all have begun with and maintained a fairly rigid, basic code of morality of some kind. One may reference Sparta, Rome, or even the British empire (Americans only but think they invented the term "hardass"). Whenever this basic code was neglected or discarded, the culture began to crumble and deteriorate. This is a well known fact of history. Either internal or external destruction (or both) was immanent. So, when Hammurabi inscribed his famous law code in honor of the Sumerian god, Shamash, he was actually only repeating and recording what was transmitted to him from those who came before, ultimately, from Adam.

The revelation God gives to men is greatly limited. We only know so much about himself as we are allowed to, by himself, and this information is also subject to his (or others) control and manipulation: spin! In fact, this is the common complaint of all unbelievers, that the only available knowledge about God has been subject to millennia of distortion and wrack-like torture to produce the distilled and marketable version that religion can control and tweak.

This explains the wild popularity of the recently discovered "lost books of revelation" that comprise the Nag-Hammadi library which were found in Egypt, in 1945. These "lost books of the Bible" many claim, comprise the "rest of the story" about God's nature, Jesus' real agenda, and so on. [It does seem a bit strange that if God could inspire a Bible, he would be inept enough to lose some of the books for nearly 2,000 years!]. In them, Jesus is portrayed as something of a mystic- magician-adept who learned his trade during the 20-some "lost years" in his life, blanked out by the four traditional gospels. During these years he is alleged to have travelled to India to learn his "magic tricks" of healing, walking on water, etc.

But if these books do not speak for God, who does claim to authoritatively represent him? Where is God's "no spin zone?" Does he have one? The Catholic Church has claimed this role for the last 2,000 years, but they can prove to be a somewhat checkered press corps, to say the least!

The problem with going toward esoteric teachings and Gnosticism, and its' modern counterpart, New Age, is that all such are very subjective in nature. At some point they all hark back to some mystical "inner light" which is different for each person. At least the Christians have "standardized" their teachings, in the form of the Apostle's Creed. All Christians adhere to this framework. No major, respected, traditional

Christian church can ignore or reject any part of this creed and still be taken seriously as an orthodox entity. But does this make the Christian faith truly objective? Hardly!

On the other hand, in esoteric systems of all kinds it's pretty much anything goes. You can introduce, integrate and incorporate about anything you want with relative impunity. To be sure, this is loads of fun: there are ouidja boards, meditation, yoga, hypnosis, tantric sex, crystals, crystal balls, bizarre midnight rituals, and you name it, it flies. But is it objective? How can you ever know if you are right about anything? Or is there even a "right?" What you end up with is the "my truth, your truth" credo. Or, the two plus two equals…whatever you want it to equal! Try to build a house with that! Is the true knowledge of God doomed to be merely a grey, amorphous miasma of uncertainty? A black hole of endless speculation? Can we ever truly know what God is really like?

If God himself is, and must ever be the only source of non-speculative revelation about himself, how can we ever know he is not "spinning" the information to favor his own agenda? And this assumes the revelation we hold (Bible) is accurate and unadulterated. How can so much evil we feel in this world, and at such a visceral level, ever be reconciled with the "beautific vision" (as the Catholics call it) of God we see presented in scripture? Are we to believe our Bibles, or our own eyes, and gut feelings? Especially when the two are at such odds? And if we are to believe the Bible, what shall we do with the candid admissions on God's part that he intentionally deceives and hardens people (as in the case of the Exodus Pharaoh, Ramses II) to facilitate their destruction? This acceptance of what we cannot see, understand, or feel is called "faith." "We walk by faith, not by sight," (2 Corinthians 5:7). Science, however, champions just the opposite: "We walk by sight, not by faith." If we can't see, touch, measure, weigh, and prove it, we reject (and often ridicule) it.

Is faith always doomed to be a mere unquestioning, credulous regurgitation of what we are told to believe? As Ronnie James Deo says in his song, *Strange Highways*, "Questions? These are forbidden. We have no answers. Believe us, anyway! ... Someone give me blessings, for they say that I have sinned..." *Who* says Ronnie has sinned? Is faith merely a spineless, supine acceptance of what we are told? Told by whom? (my – that is faith!) Would you buy a house this way?

So has Metallica finally called out the Wizard? Has our little Toto dog of investigation uncovered a perjurer? A scoundrel of deception? Will he float away in a space balloon to another Kansas-like universe if we expose him? If so, how then shall we rightly navigate this witch infested Oz without him?

We contend that our Men of Metal have, at the very least, performed a valuable service to century 21 U.S.A. They have challenged the Christians to a rebuttal. They accuse God of being a cruel, capricious, bloodletting control freak... a master of puppets! And don't look now, but *you* are one of those puppets! (You live here don't you?)

And even more unsettling is the fact that the Bible, at least in part, supports these allegations.

Consider common sense, reason, experience, and history. All these can be brought to the bar to accuse God.

Consider the witness of conscience. Yes, my conscience may tell me I'm wrong if I lie, cheat, steal, or kill. But, does it not also rise up when I see a dead baby, a suffering child, a cop who kills and gets paid for it, a crooked judge, a senator who gets wealthy by lying, stealing from, and cheating the people who elected him (true, there are a couple who don't do this)? And all this is done with the apparent approval of God? Consider also nature. Is there not something inherently evil about the never flagging, shear cruelty of the natural order? Dog eats vomit, dog eats feces, dog eats dog…(and you let that thing lick your face?) And if believers object by saying that in the original creation God never intended for nature to be so vicious, or animals so cruel, we have to ask, "Then, why did he create lions with such big teeth, powerful paws, claws, if they were meant to eat grass…?"

Unfortunately, most Christians have never bothered to carry out the implications of their faith to anywhere near as fine a point as these fearless young musicians have done. It seems the same three witnesses to the righteous nature of God: Creation, Scripture, and Conscience also take the stand to accuse him! But who will judge the Judge? Who can arraign the highest authority in the universe? And in which court? The celebrated patriarch Abraham himself broached this thought when he asked a very penetrating, howbeit rhetorical question, "Shall not the Judge of all the earth do right?" And what is even more amazing is that in the course of this bizarre negotiation (found in Genesis 18) on behalf of the non-destruction of the notorious cities of Sodom and Gomorrha, God, in the form of his special envoy (some claim this mysterious figure was actually Jesus, before his incarnation, and "incognito") actually acquiesced! He allowed Abraham to "bargain him down" from 50 to a mere 10 souls (he would go no lower). So, apparently God is sensitive to being probed on this matter… (?)

Does he not rather suspiciously swat down any objections to his purpose in Romans 9:20? Does not Paul ask in God's stead, "Shall the thing formed say to him that formed it, why has thou made me thus?" Peter, in his second book, 2:12, refers to certain people as "natural brute beasts, made to be taken (captured) and destroyed…" So, apparently God does create some people for the mere purpose of destruction, both their own, and the others they influence (reference Mr. Hitler, among others). "The Lord hath made all things for himself, yea even the wicked for the day of evil," (Proverbs 16:4), or in a bitterly debated scripture in Isaiah, "That they may know from the rising of the sun, and from the west (!) that there is none beside me. I am the LORD, and there is none else. I form the light, and create darkness (spiritual as well as actual): I make peace, and create evil: I the LORD do all these things… (45:6-7). One can also note the air of bravado, almost boasting that God expresses here as he quite shamelessly takes on full responsibility for his creation, and the sometimes dark results that accrue from it… A righteous Creator need fear none, or cringe at the scrutiny of his subordinates… If you don't like it, you can go…where? To hell of course!

Is it, will it be any surprise, if, on the day of judgement the non-elect, not chosen person should ask the only reasonable question he could ask, "Why did you create me? You knew what I would be…" What would *you* ask? (or perhaps more frighteningly, what *will* you ask?!). And isn't it strange that this is the one very question the querist is forbidden to ask in Romans 9:20?

In the movie Con Air, when the naughty rapist is being

thwarted by the hero he asks, "What do you think I am?" And the whimsical response is, "Ugly all day..." Only here, the sinner faces the unsavory prospect of being "ugly all eternity..."

Or in the story of Pinnochio, when the wooden hero lands on Donkey Island, and gradually realizes that he is being slowly, but irrevocably transformed into a jackass, it gives him pause, and he eventually decides to change course... Only this Donkey Island is eternal, and the choice to devolve was made without our consent, before we were ever born! Ouch!

So once more we must ask, has the curtain been pulled back to reveal the true nature of "the wicked Wizard of the West?"

CHAPTER SEVEN
THE PROBLEMS

The first problem: If the Satanists, or faith rejecters are right, how then do we explain good? Why is there good in the world?

The second problem: If the Christians are right, how then do we explain not only evil and suffering, but the fact that God, by his own admission deceives people to their own destruction? Worse still, that in the future he is prepared to launch a massive, world-wide delusion that will result in destruction and damnation on an immense scale.

In addition you have to go back to the beginning, and ask about the origins of this whole mess. Chaos was introduced, injected into the universe by a thought, then a choice by Lucifer (unless you like the Zoroastrian model, in which case the destroyer is Ahriman). God did nothing to prevent this. In fact, he enabled it. Why? God placed three infinitely volatile ingredients together in one place (the Garden of Eden) at one time (the opening days after creation). In this way the chaos was massively replicated, and multiplied. If you exclude the tree (of the knowledge of good and evil), the man (Adam), or the snake (Lucifer) there could have been no fall of man, no sinful human race to redeem in the first place. As with the components of an explosive, leave just one out, and no boom. So here. Yet, this omniscient Chemist chose to include all three. Why? Adam was so innocent, so naïve that he did not even know he was naked. How could he possibly have fathomed the astonishing implications of his action? Yet God chose to not only hold him accountable, but all his progeny, and not only for the temporal and physical, but also the eternal and spiritual repercussions of his action. Is that really justice? If you put a child in a room full of toys and grenades, would *you* not be held responsible if he managed to deconstruct himself? Would you hold his (potential) offspring responsible for both the liability, and the mess? For the next 6,000 years? And, should any of us (Adam's now culpable descendants) object to this colossal, cosmic, forensic smash and grab, to whom are we to appeal? To further complicate this, we have a notoriously meager stock of information about both the fall of Adam, and the fall of Lucifer. We just simply are not given many details about either event, and these two events are arguably the two most pivotal in all human history.

We contend, at this point that the analogy of puppets gets the idea across, but is not perhaps the best one. It is more like the "master of puppets" is actually a producer/director who is managing a tight, complex script. We have more freedom than puppets, but each of us seems to have been handed a script which we are powerless to refuse to read from. We are allowed to "ad lib" a bit, but to change the storyline, we cannot. The musician and lyricist, Jim Morrison of The Doors used this metaphor when he sang, "… into this house we're born, into this world we're thrown, like a dog without a bone, an actor out of loan, riders on the storm…" Upon examination, we contend that we do actually have some choice in all this, but it is reduced to two choices, and only two. We can choose to be "unwillingly willing," as the Christians will say. Or, we can choose to be "willingly unwilling," and assume the role of traitors and rebels (pirates, really) in the form of "unrepentant sinners." So we can choose which of the two roles we will fulfill… and yet, now we are told that even this choice is really not ours after all!

Another kink in this chain is what we call the "shotgun bride" concept. This is where God's offer in the gospel can be looked upon as essentially the same thing as a "shotgun wedding!" The lost sinner is given the following simple ultimatum: "repent or perish." Neat, huh? Why, a feller could fill a whole stadium full of good looking wives with this expedient! "Either you marry me, right now, or I blow your brains out." Only in this case the discharge of the shotgun is not just for a bloody instant, but an eternal blast of relentless, merciless fury and torment……
The prospective bride (that is, *you*) can either stubbornly face down the gun and wait for the inevitable damning blast, or you can "chose" to accept the "loving" gospel invitation initiated by your prospective beau, Jesus. "There's room at the cross for you……" But, is that really a choice? Also, the prospective bride is offered, in this world at least, what? Mansions? A lovely beach honeymoon? No, sorry, dear. A cross of your own! In fact, Jesus stridently declares, over and over, that if you are not willing to

be "crucified with Christ" you are worthy of neither him, his salvation, or his future kingdom! In simple language that is, "Be crucified, or go to hell."

Did Jesus, the gentle Shepherd really present the gospel in this harsh way? Afraid so. In Luke 13:1-3, upon considering those poor Jews whose blood Pilate had mingled with their own temple animal sacrifices, Jesus said, " I tell you ... except you repent, you shall all likewise perish." And so they did, in 70 A.D. during the brutal fall of Jerusalem to Rome. Jesus wasn't kidding. In this case he was specifically addressing first century Jews, but any Christian will tell you that this same constraint to repent holds true to this day. Now, do believers ever complain about this rough treatment by their future "husband" (the Church is referred to repeatedly in scripture as the Bride of Christ)? Have you ever heard one do so? Apparently they think *any* wedding is better than none, or else they have never thought the whole thing quite through... We tend to assume the latter, that most believers are so sluggish that they just bit right into the prepackaged gospel happy meal they were offered without ever bothering to examine the label to see what ingredients it might contain... The Berean Christians of Acts 17 were "more noble" than this, but who has time for such an irksome task today? There are football games to watch, Big Macs to eat, roller coasters to ride, and thank God, beer to drink... (!)

Is the Bible and Calvinist theology verifying what Metallica has charged? In a way, they are. Is Metallica preaching the gospel? In a way, they are presenting the gospel from "the dark side," something like when you are at the bottom of a pool, and see a person standing by the side. Everything they are saying is true, with one debatable exception, which is the intrinsic character of

God. They charge him with being an evil, cruel "puppet master," while the Bible and the Christian faith regard him as the "gentle shepherd." But there is yet another problem, and this one is a doozy!

The third problem: the cross. Talk about "this changes everything...!" This highly unreasonable and totally illogical event throws a monkey wrench into any possible examination into these questions. No amount of on-field review, or multiplicity of camera angles can ever render this problem clear, and obvious. It appears Jesus became a puppet also! Only his hands and feet were not secured by strings, but by large nails! Spikes! Yikes! And, as a puppet must perform the actions dictated by the Master, so he repeatedly affirmed that he "came not to do his own will, but the will of his Father..." And, one has to admit, no matter WHAT accusations can be leveled against it, the gospel, the cross is a nice idea. It has supernal elements and themes of love, giving and devotion that are entirely without parallel in non-Biblical literature. In effect, it has never been excelled! What story surpasses the fabulous epic of a creator who becomes his own creation, and willingly dies the most brutal death human imagination could invent, purely out of love for them, and his Father?? As the Christmas hymn "O Holy Night" cantors,

> "Long lay the world in sin and error pining
> 'Till *he* appeared, and the soul felt its' worth...
> A thrill of hope, the weary world rejoices,
> For yonder breaks a new, and glorious morn..."

Are you, am I *that* valuable, that precious to God? Is that possible? It is a sublime notion, and clearly one that should never be taken lightly, or marginalized, no matter what one may ultimately do with it... Even if it turns out to be false, or fictional, it is still an awesome and uplifting concept that, pound for pound will probably never be transcended in human thought, music, or literature...

The point we wish to make here is not to call in question the veracity of the historical happening known as the cross/resurrection. It is possibly the most well supported event of antiquity. It has an abundance of corroborating evidence, from a plethora of sources. We wish rather to call in question the fundamental motive and impelling purpose behind the event. Why did God send his son? The Bible reason is given as follows:

> "God sent not his son into the world to condemn the world, but that the world through him might be saved. He that believeth on him is not condemned. He that believeth not is condemned already... and this is the condemnation, that light is come into the world but men loved darkness rather than light, because their deeds were evil..."

The world was already condemned. Not all the world will be saved. Many will never even hear the gospel. Many died before there was a gospel. If Calvin, Luther, and Jonathan Edwards are right (and these are three of the most prominent theologians the Protestants have: the reformation was largely based on the work of two of them), multitudes are spiritually incapable of responding to the message, and cannot be saved. So, why indeed did God send his son? If the reason was "that the world through him might be saved," it appears to have been a failed mission.

CHAPTER EIGHT
THE OPTIONS

Or, "The Outs"

In the movie "Heat," Jon Voight gives Robert DeNiro his "out." This is the getaway he will use, once the "job" (the bank heist, or whatever is brewing) is over. Well, good reader, pay attention, because here are your "outs," and there are not very many. You will be required to choose one (yes, there is going to be a test!).

Out number one: You can "accept Jesus as your personal savior," as any Christian will be more than happy to walk you through. Whether you do it by eating him, as in the Catholic mass, or just "praying him into your heart," as the Protestants will instruct, or by getting into the water (which about all of them will want you to do), it is one sure-fire way to avoid hell, and be covered, no matter what the economy decides to do.

Out number two: You can hope the Eastern dualists are right, and try to become worthy of being assimilated into the "universal one-mind," the cosmic energy field known as Nirvana, Satori, Brahman, etc. If you do accomplish this, you will have yourself to thank for your own deliverance and eternal felicity. Since Buddhism is an intrinsically atheistic system, you won't have to be tethered by God's existence, if you choose to go that route. You may have to endure thousands of painful reincarnations in the process, but, hey, it's worth it. Right?

Out number three: You can forget the whole mess and simply embrace the fact that you are nothing more than another meaningless monkey waiting for the melancholy meltdown of extinction to place you on the ever growing, putrefying heap of evolving former species. Those who follow you will take your place by climbing up on this writhing mass of defunct prototypes, and so go another notch higher toward...what? Basically, nothing! This, too, is a purely atheistic system of thought, so there is no sticky, religious syrup to wade through (or be baptized in).

If the evolutionary scenario is true, you may as well go ahead and have a good laugh at the utter futility and nihilistic meaninglessness of your own existence. "This Bud's for you!" Drink up, and have a good laugh at this joke because *you are the punchline*! In Michael Chrichton's "The Lost World," the fictional character Ian Malcom, a strident evolutionist, states, "What makes you think human beings are sentient, and aware? There is no evidence for it. Human beings never think for themselves, they find it too uncomfortable. For the most part, members of our species simply repeat what they are told... We are stubborn, self-destructive conformists. Any other view of our species is just self congratulatory delusion..." Thank you, Dr. Malcom...

Out number four: You can purchase a small prayer carpet,

and obtain a GPS fix upon, and shoot an azimuth toward Mecca (this is located in central Arabia). You will need to be prepared to rise at around 4:00 am each morning for your first prayer of the day to Allah. It may also be helpful to take up Arabic. An alternative to this is that you can lobby for the rebuilding of the Jewish temple in Jerusalem. You may also need to obtain a small prayer shawl, and/or a skull cap. In either of these two systems you will have an almighty deity with whom you will be able to find favor, if you maintain the proscribed deeds, rituals, and beliefs. When the time comes, he will be pleased to reward you in proportion to your careful adherence to the correct dogma.

Out number five: You can hope that your dark horse, Lucifer (or Ahriman?), will mastermind a magnificent upset. He may yet stage a stunning coup d'etat, and overthrow God. Never mind Revelation 12-20. Those prophecies were produced by the incumbent heavenly administration, and as such are subject to the correlating spin. Heavenly spin, if you will. Not left wing, or west wing, but "angel-wing" spin! Here is something Mr. O'Reilly has not covered yet!

In Calvinist theology there is not now, and there never has been any serious competition between God and Lucifer. The Puritans went so far as to relegate Lucifer (whom they would call "Satan") to the level of being "God's ape." For them, it was all settled before it ever began, and all that really remains is for this mega-movie to finish playing, so we can all read the credits. But, is this really true? If Zarathustra (Zoroaster), the Cathars, the Manicheans, the Satanists, Gnostics and New Agers everywhere (and throughout history, beginning in the Garden of Eden) are right, this may not be a done deal yet! Zoroaster was perhaps the first to propound the idea that God and Ahriman are rivals that are, right now, fighting over control of the world, and especially over the souls of men. God is ahead right now, but only slightly, as in a tightly fought OU-Texas game... He said that God (Ormazd) would win, but hey...

Most would agree that at times it does almost seem that the powers of good are teetering on the edge of defeat. It almost seems that the dark side is winning, the nice guys are coming in last, and that this zoo story is anything but over. During the Battle for Britain in World War II, for those who languished and died in German or Russian camps, or the walkers of the Bataan death march it may have seemed so. For murder and rape victims, and multitudes of others who know injustice at a visceral level, it must seem so. Those buried under tons of rubble in the fall of the World Trade Center, or those who jumped from windows to escape the fire within, in their last seconds might have said or thought so. Their loved ones who had to eulogize them may have thought it. And who could blame them?

It is natural for us as humans to simply ignore the existence of evil, until we are confronted with it on a personal, direct basis. Like Neo in "The Matrix", we will try to dodge this bullet for as long as possible. If the evil we see, feel, or experience is overwhelming enough, it is indeed easy to begin to wonder which "side" is really in charge, or winning.

CHAPTER NINE
THE CONCLUSIONS

The man who is supposed to be the wisest who ever lived said, "Let us hear the conclusion of the whole matter..." This after 12 chapters of pontificating upon the futility of life in general, and pondering some of the same issues we have nibbled on in this little book. His final answer is, "Fear God and keep his commandments, for this the whole duty of man..." (Ecclesiastes 12:13-14). Thanks, Schlomo (Solomon), but we may need a bit more...

Regardless of the existence of some "eternal decree," you and I must, right here, right now choose to believe something. I don't know about you, but I want to believe the truth. The problem with this is obvious. Pilate asked Jesus, "What is truth?" Unfortunately, he did not wait around long enough to hear an answer (a fairly common practice). On another occasion Jesus said to his Father, "Thy word is truth." Of course Jesus would tell us the Bible, the gospel is the truth. He was, however, hardly an unbiased reporter. So the question remains, what is truth, or the truth? Shall we follow our own "inner light?" Or seek an external source of truth? In the end, you will either have to concoct your own recipe, or take somebody's word for it.

We thought about asking all these questions, and then just signing off, and leaving the answer for you, good reader, to figure out. But, since it is rude to present a problem without even an attempt at a solution, we will here present for your consideration some conclusions we have arrived at. These were conceived in hours of careful cogitation, prayer, and with the assistance of some of the finest writings, Bibles, commentaries, and the best whiskies and cigars known to man.

CONCLUSIONS: One: There is good in the world.

Two: The world did not get here all by itself. If Lucifer did not create it (as he never claims to have done),God must have put it here.

Three: An evil creator would not create anything good. He would have created a world with only evil. We would be "born in hell." The good I perceive is not a delusion. It could be, and I might never know for sure until after I die, but frankly, I doubt it.

Four: It seems incontrovertible that if you adopt a Calvinistic theological view that God is clearly a "master of puppets," if you are among the number of the non-elect. If you are among the elect, he is still a master of puppets, howbeit with the salutary inclusion that he is a benign, benevolent master, but a master nonetheless! (So! Our boys were right, after all!)

Five: It does not make sense that God would create a being

that could "kick his ass." Therefore, Lucifer cannot possibly win. How could an omnipotent being ever be defeated, or outsmarted? It makes better sense that Lucifer actually believes he can defeat God (more on this later), and that he actively recruits others to hold this belief.

Six: If the Bible is not true, then we have no idea of what God is truly like, in any detail. True or not, we can never prove it either way. This is by design. God preferred to set up a system where we are each required to approach him strictly on the basis of faith. For some reason, he seems to really like this thing we call "faith."

Seven: Jesus would not have died for a "P.R. stunt." Compliance through deception would not be necessary for an evil deity, and would be reprehensible to a righteous one. If, however, in the process of "redeeming" people (which literally means to buy or purchase), Jesus enslaves and tyrannizes them, one must question his motives somewhat...

Eight: The "drama of redemption" would be a dull story indeed if you omitted the fall of Adam, and Lucifer. It would be not so much a "drama" as an episode of "Ozzie and Harriett on Seroquel" (both you and them). We would all be quiescently planting roses and tending orange trees in the much expanded Garden of Eden. There would be no weeds to pull. Lions and tigers would eat grass. The angels would probably all be asleep. (More on this in "The Process," which follows).

In the movie, "The Watchmen," the god-like character called "Dr. Manhatten," who has received quasi-supernatural powers and intelligence through a strange accident, postulates the existence of the world as it would be without human life.

He comments upon how peaceful, simple, and pristine such a humanless world would be, and asks if such a state might not be preferable to this one. All this is induced by a painful breakup with his former, ravishing girlfriend. He even opts to "move out" to another entire galaxy to live, preferring the accommodations there to here. Which, of course, brings up an interesting point. Suppose God, as the blue-skinned Dr. did, had determined that human life was an annoying, redundant waste of time? Would the universe, God's ultimate glory, and all parties concerned, be better off without humans ever having been here? Apparently not (Hooray! We exist! I guess, as the makeup commercial alleges, we are "worth it").

Nine: Slave-like compliance with God's will surely does not please him. Apparently God likes "a little whiskey in his coffee…" Some of the people in the Bible who seem to have been most used and loved by God had a fairly ragged individual case history… (reference David, Samson, Rahab, Joab, Jacob, Jonah!). It remains to be seen exactly how much fun (or adventure, or latitude, or something) one can have and still remain within the parameters of God's approval…

Ten: We really do not know much about the fall of either Adam, or Lucifer. Both are (obviously) pivotal events. Assuming God was righteous in each case, then we truly are at his mercy (just as Calvin said), and the "smart money" would be on seeking this mercy. With the limited information we have, we are really not in a position to make a very comprehensive evaluation of these questions. This relegates our conclusions to the realm of conjecture. Even if you could sit down with God, interview and interrogate him, in the end you would have to decide whether or not to believe what he told you. You would have to judge God, and make a referee-like call as to his personal character and nature. Is any human really qualified to do this? And yet, each of us, at some point, is required to do *exactly* this. This is what is being done every time a preacher presents the gospel, only we are not sitting across the kitchen table, looking Jesus in the eye, as we sip a cup of coffee, and wonder if he's telling the truth...

Eleven: It only makes sense that the only way to know and guarantee the outcome of any event is to control it at every pivotal point of development. If God controls the loss of scalp hair, and the death of sparrows, it is unlikely that human (or any other) freewill can ever contravene his purpose. This pretty much kills off any talk of "process..." (to be discussed later).

Twelve: God actually (and almost violently) forces each of us to do two things, and only two things, really. First, we are forced to be born, and become a part of this slave camp, the unfolding saga of life here on "Planet Dirt." Second, we are forced to choose to believe something. We have no choice about either one of those. Every other event, thought, or feeling we will ever experience is based upon these two things. We cannot refuse to be born, and we cannot refuse to believe something. (Even if one were to chose to believe "nothing," that in itself is a belief system called nihilism.)

I do not at all like the idea that I have been conscripted to be an actor, or puppet. I also do not like being a highly evolved, howbeit, meaningless primate. I do not like the idea of burning forever, but must admit that I do somewhat like the role of rebel or pirate. At least as a pirate and spiritual mutineer, I *feel* like I am in control of my own destiny, and there are certain perks to the job (no income tax, endless supply of rum, beach front property, etc.)!

Thirteen: It seems utterly impossible to conclude otherwise than that, at least in some form, God and Lucifer are symbionts. It may be true that Satan feeds on the misery and suffering that humans experience from day to day. But, is this not also true of God? If not, then why would he base the redemption of his entire universe on the basis of the suffering of his son, his servants, his martyrs, etc.? Why would the entire Christian paradigm continually refer back to this tragic, bloody event (the cross), and "feed" off the energy of it, as well as the countless other stories and testimonies of the sufferings endured by his people throughout history?

Chapter Ten
The Prestige

In a recent movie entitled "The Prestige," that stars Hugh Jackman and Christian Bale, the two competing magicians each force their audience to accept the fact that they are doing something that is impossible. They present two opposites that cannot both be true at the same time. In the case of Bale, his character has a secret identical twin that renders his trick an illusion. Jackman's trick is, by means of a secret machine, not a trick. He is actually reproducing himself, and the audience is really seeing two of him at the same time, though one is quickly disposed of.

We here submit that God is presenting to us a "prestige," the conclusion of a magic trick that forces us to accept the impossible.

Here are a few of the impossible opposites that God has created, and that we must somehow accept:

1. God vs. Man. Jesus, in his incarnation is both God, and man.
2. Freewill vs. Predestination. We were chosen, yet must choose.
3. Infusion of grace vs. Imputation of grace. We cannot earn salvation, yet must.
4. Mercy vs. Hell. God is merciful, yet upon some, shows no mercy.
5. Good vs. Evil. God created the potential for evil, yet he is not evil.
6. Human sacrifice vs. not. God forbids human sacrifice, yet performs one.
7. Love vs. Curse. God loves the world, yet cursed it soon after creation.

This list could be extended indefinitely (and the longer it got, the more indefinite it would become). When people say the Bible is full of contradictions, they are right.

"The inside of the stomach is on the outside of the body." This enigmatic quote is from my high school science teacher, Mr. Thomas. He told us to go home and ponder this, and come back and explain why we did or did not agree with it. Of course, I challenged him on it, and said it was absurd. But, maybe Mr. Thomas was right. Consider the following…

Somehow, God has managed to do (again!) what to our eyes is impossible. He has created evil without ever becoming contaminated by it. Food starts out clean, pure, and nourishing. Once it is ingested, it undergoes a bizarre transformation. During the process life is sustained and made possible, yet the food is sacrificed. It becomes fecal material: reeking, rancid, and disgusting. It can be buried and used as fertilizer (which again, supports more growth, more life), but is otherwise something to be patently avoided. Sin and Satan are like the food the universe feeds upon. And somehow, God has allowed that the believing may receive sustenance from this, one-time pure, now toxic mix, yet, without contamination. Satan and evil are like the negative post of a battery, or the south pole of a magnet.

Here is, we think, the true, basic nature of pure evil. Evil is a form of insanity that attempts to do what can only be done by God himself: to create reality. In this case to create a separate and distinct reality that is apart from and contradictory to (or at best, parallel to) the one and only one that is. *That* reality is *this* one, and no other. Just as Jesus is and can only ever be the only savior, he can only be the savior of this reality. There are no other "dimensions," universes, or worlds. Strangely, some of the most brilliant modern astro-physicists have begun to postulate just this possibility...

In Ray Bradbury's "Illustrated Man," one of the tattoos has Jesus travelling the universe on a planet-hopping evangelistic tour, saving souls. The problem with this is simply that it is not likely to be true. Jesus only died once, and that was here on Earth, in Jerusalem, Israel. If there are any living inhabitants of other planets, either they are getting a "second hand" gospel about a savior who died on another planet, or else they never sinned, and need no savior This is, of course, not impossible, but is never mentioned in scripture, and just sounds really weird.

CHAPTER ELEVEN
THE PROCESS

The well known and little loved figure Charles Manson is a nut case, to be sure. Yet he is certainly not without a twisted brilliance. At some point in his life he was profoundly influenced by two distinctive religious teachings: Scientology, and a lesser known school of thought called "Process Theology" (though anyone connected to either group would denounce him today).

Scientology was founded by the science fiction writer L. Ron Hubbard, and is well known for attracting to its' fold many Hollywood luminaries. Compared to the major orthodox Christian denominations extant, and their traditional teachings, it is "out there." But it is just a warm-up compared to Process thinking.

In a word, Process theology teaches that, so far from being ultimately enemies in conflict, competing for the prize of the control of the universe, the souls of men, the destiny of angels, etc., that God and Lucifer are actually more like symbiont organisms each complementing the purpose and intent of the other. Thus history is a "process" of the ultimate resolution of this cooperation. God created Lucifer because he needed him, and could not possibly have done the job without his input, and in effect, assistance. Not so much in a sense of weakness, but it was more like necessity. It does not make a table weak because it requires legs to stand, it is just in the nature of the table. God designed his creation in such a way that the interactions of this dark assistant were required. A belief system held by the Yazidis of Iraq, of Kurdish ancestry, hold many ideas that concur with this idea, and descend loosely from the Zoroastrian faith. They revere "Melek Taus," the Peacock God.

Yet, as with the many other contradictory themes we find in scripture, God is in no way besmirched by this setup. He remains pristine and spotless, but uses "Lucy" (as I call him) in the same way a master mechanic uses his Snap-on ratchet, or an artist uses his brush. A simple illustration is found in the familiar: reproduction. Neither male nor female are weak or lacking, yet each requires the input of the other to accomplish this notable achievement, without which, it would be impossible.

This thought in mind, you can apply this concept to virtually all New Age, Gnostic, and Dualist teachings, along with many other non-Christian (or non-monotheistic) systems. Like Yin and Yang (an idea that perfectly comports with this) these two superminds perform an ongoing ballet of act and react which jets through history like a firework in flight. This is precisely the kind of thing that got the Templars in trouble, that many of the heretics were burned for (the Cathari, e.g.), and that may have even motivated to some extent the thinking of Judas Iscariot to do what he did.

It is also not entirely incompatible with monotheism, as the Jewish Kabbalah, as well as the sect of Islam known as Sufism which very much embraces mystical teachings which embody this sort of concept quite well. In fact, virtually all Occultic and arcane teachings that exist are one or other twist off this licorice stick (black licorice, of course!). Hence, there is a vast body of material to support it, but mostly "dark side" stuff, also called "left hand path."

Unfortunately for Orthodox theology, there is a shocking amount of scripture, if one prefers to interpret it this way, to support this. Some of these passages have already been alluded to above. Another example is the well known idea of a "scapegoat," or "azazel" as he is called in the Hebrew. This unfortunate beast was given the astringent task of bearing away the burden of the sin of Israel. Upon it the elders "dumped" the confessed sin of the nation. It was then sent away into the wilderness "by the hand of a fit man." The animal (Leviticus 16) was always a he-goat! This is precisely the creature of choice to depict Lucifer in much popular literature! In Satanic motifs a goat's head superimposed over a downward pointing pentagram is a common way of representing Lucy.

Another is the account of Jesus' temptation in the desert. Why was it necessary to check in with this master villain before he could begin to save the souls of men? Why does Lucy have ready access to, not only heaven, but God's very presence? And why is he allowed to "change policy" as we see in the account found in Job's first chapter? Why was he admitted entrance to the Garden of Eden in the first place? Why allowed to "enter into the heart of Judas Iscariot" at a critical moment in redemptive history? Why did Moses lift up a serpent in the wilderness? Why not a cat, or something? Why did Jesus feel compelled to refer back to this event in the magnificently redemptive third chapter of John? And from this account is based the worldwide symbol of medical healing: the caduceus, or serpent suspended from a cross! (All, right, all right, we can argue the point if it is one snake or two, wings, or not, cross, or simple staff, caduceus, or rod of Asclepius... but this author will allege that the Mosaic event of Numbers 21 preceded all of the above, and they are all based upon this occurrence). This whole event just reads like a magic spell, and has powerful occultic implications.

Time and again one can lift right from the very pages of scripture actions and statements that would make a fairly strong argument for complicity in, say, a murder case, if it were known that a party allowed a certain participant to be present on frequent occasions of questionable and critical outcome.

In a sense, isn't that what human history is? Is it not an unending train of ebb and flow, light versus dark, good against evil? To suggest that God is somehow in complicity with Lucifer in all this is a stretch, no doubt. Yet, it does make one wonder why "the fallen one" is even permitted to be in the steering house of the ship, if he is never meant, however briefly, to take the wheel...

And, since God is an omnipotent and almighty deity, is it possible that Lucifer's original love for him was so intense that he was virtually compelled to accept this murky role, realizing that it was simply a dirty job that no one else could possibly have done with the panache and superbly blazing skill set that he has, clearly, brought to the task? A most bizarre, yet striking love story?

As in the recently popular movie trilogy based on the brilliantly intense and intricate suspense and action novels authored by Robert Ludlum, the "Bourne" series, the "hero" is of dubious origin. He is persuaded, out of love for his country, to voluntarily assume the role of assassin, and cold blooded, conscienceless killer. In his case, there is an excruciatingly difficult, but possible window for reversal of this dark purpose. In the case of Lucifer, however, no redemption, forgiveness, or return would ever be possible. Would this not be a kind of love that even Jesus himself could not exceed? If so, then who is the greater savior? Could it be that the infinite inequity of these two roles is the basis for the famous rage that Satan in so known for?

It gets weird, doesn't it?

CHAPTER TWELVE
THE APPEARANCE

If it be true that God himself is bound by certain self-imposed parameters, namely his own word and nature (Heb 6), this changes dramatically the possible perception of him being guilty of tyranny. He is not exactly free to just do "whatever." Yet, paradoxically, it is also still true that "God is in the heavens: he hath done whatsoever he hath pleased" (Psalm 115:3). His nature would require of him to do all that he does for the greatest possible ultimate good, and in the best possible way it could be done. Good and better would not be options. This would limit every possible eventuality to only one possible outcome: the best one. We call this concept "single outcome potentiality." To say again, God himself has no choice but to cause/allow things to turn out only one possible way. *Only one way.*

God has no alternative but to allow things to appear to be a certain way, when in reality they are not. We will call this the "necessity of appearance." If one takes the Bible seriously when it uses the word "predestination," there is no room for luck or fate. Though this kind of talk is extremely unpopular in this freewill exalting culture, it is nonetheless either true, or not. The Bible does not limit the providential control of creation to those events regarding the salvation of men. It militates in favor of the idea that God controls every aspect of his creation, and manages it with the most meticulous care and oversight. And, he has done so since the beginning, and continues to do so now. This arrangement will never change (oops!).

For example, every game to be played, football or baseball, has already been determined as to who shall win. It only *appears* that the outcome is in question. Since we humans do not yet know what this predetermined outcome is, it is incumbent upon us to follow out a trail to see where it will lead, though from God's perspective the outcome is already settled.

It is not God's purpose to deceive us in this setup. He has, in effect, no choice but to do it this way to conform to the laws of nature which he himself established. It was not his intention to deceive Jeremiah, mentioned above, either. The same rules applied there as here. It is very unfortunate that at certain times, some people are subjected to considerable suffering as a result of this fact (see "The Burn," later).

If we knew ahead of time the outcome of an action, we might be inclined to refuse to act, or to act differently than we do. We act based upon our immediate perception of the way to achieve the best or most desirable outcome.

Jonathan Edwards, the brilliant, and famous colonial era Puritan thinker, author, and theologian touches on a similar idea in his treatise upon freewill. He contends that as humans, we are so subject to our immediate perception of what we want, or think is best for us, that in reality we do not have freewill at all. When one factors in the belief in "total depravity" (as Edwards believed), it is entirely plausible that Edwards could be right. This brings us back to the idea of us being no more than "actors upon a stage" playing out a script.

Another aspect of this idea, and one that necessarily and obviously follows is the "necessity of silence/secrecy." God could not reveal aspects of the future, or his "secret will" (as the Puritans called it) without entirely disrupting both the flow of history, and his own purpose. He has to remain silent about some things, at least for the time being. Even on a human level, parents are familiar with this. We simply cannot tell our children everything we know, because they could not handle it, or they would be harmed by the knowledge. No harmful, but rather a protective intent is present.

History is a "closed system." Nothing can be added, or taken out. Even though all outcomes (all events really) are controlled and settled already, each event must still take place, in order, to allow for the one that follows, something like grains of sand passing through an hour glass…cars connected in a train…lines of code in a computer program…

As a sperm cell travels from its' source to its' target, with the potentiality of creating a new, eternal being, so here. The moment the deity chose to create, he set in motion a series of parameters that culminate in this present reality. Being himself voluntarily limited by his own choices and nature, the principle of "single outcome potentiality" required of him to do the only thing he, in his foreknowledge determined could be done. And, with the bare guarantee of his promise and pledge, and no greater proof or evidence than creation, scripture, and the cross, we must choose to endorse or oppose this divine program...

And, as the human body's least honored (yea, most dishonored) members are those solely capable of eternal potentiality in the sense of creating human life, perhaps God chooses to use the seemingly least honored means to carry forward his most noble purposes.

Chapter Thirteen
The Burn

Or, "Why We Suffer"

Good ol' Marines, and their sayings. They have one that is well known: "No pain, no gain." Previously, we looked at the problem of suffering, which has been "looked at" for thousands of years. No doubt, minutes after Cain murdered his little brother, his parents began to wonder about this. The question is examined in the well known book of Job. Rabbi Harold Kushner wrote about it in his notable book, "Why Bad Things Happen to Good People."

Suffering, misery, and pain of all kinds have characterized the human race since its' inception. So why does the loving, "white" monotheist God of the Christian faith allow, yea, foment all this agony? Does he like it? Well, fasten your seatbelt, dear reader, because here is the accurate, Biblical answer: Yes. He does.

Let's take a look at one of the most loved, hated, debated, and quoted chapters of the Bible, Isaiah 53. In this famous passage, the "arm of the LORD," known and agreed upon to be the Messiah, is shown to suffer. In fact, this very fact is the principle one that caused the Jewish Sanhedrin, the leaders of the nation of Israel, to reject Jesus as their Messiah. They simply could not square his role of a suffering, peaceful, spiritual "savior" with the many, very clear prophesies in the Old Testament about the military, economic, and political nature of the kingdom he was supposed to bring about. They wanted no part of a suffering messiah. Even Jesus' own disciples stumbled upon this point. Peter himself drew a sword to defend Jesus when a party of armed men came to arrest him on that historic night in the garden. It was not until after the resurrection that they began, slowly, to realize that, for now, a spiritual kingdom was all they were going to get. The rest would come later; much later (about 2,000 years now, and counting!). No one living today should blame these Jews for not "getting it." If we today were faced with anything like such a bewildering departure from the expected, predicted norm, we would likely fare no better, possibly much worse.

This "suffering of Christ" that the Christians speak and preach so much about, what was it?

Well, you know the story and the gory: the spikes, the whip, the thorns, tears, spears, etc., etc. Thank you, Mel Gibson. We might never have gotten it, if it weren't for you. But is this bloody ordeal the thing that "saves sinners?" Was it all entirely necessary? Which part of this debacle was the real heart of the atonement (a contrived word from the words at-one-ment)?

According to the most soaring, poetic account of the incident in scripture, as penned by Isaiah, strangely a full seven and a half centuries before the fact, the most important aspect of the crucifixion of Christ was not the nails. It was not the whip. Not the thorns. Not the post-mortem spear. No, *not even the blood*. Isaiah avers that it was the *emotional aspect* of the atonement that is the core event that springs the sinner from his condemnation, and speeds him to the heart of God's pardon, grace, and love. Isaiah tells us in verse 11: "He shall see the travail of his soul, and be satisfied…" The person being satisfied is God. The satisfaction is speaking of the appeasement of the anger and rage that God has experienced, and, for the most part, refrained from acting upon, since the first sin was ever committed up to this time. Though, on occasion (reference Genesis 6-8, the account of the Noahic flood) God has allowed himself to vent his wrath, mostly, he has held it in until this day, when he poured it all out upon his own son. The next installment of this will be the apocalypse…

It was this internal agony of Christ, this realization that for a brief time the eternal love-bond between Father and Son was not only broken, but completely ruptured, that was the extreme culmination and climax of this milestone known as the "cross," or the atonement. This is the "travail (agony, or torture) of soul" being referred to. And this explains why Jesus sweat, not bullets, but drops of blood hours before, in mental and emotional anticipation of the pain that was soon to follow. This is why Jesus was so bummed with his disciples in the garden of Gethsemane. They were entirely clueless as to the magnitude of what was about to unfold, though he had warned them about it over and over ahead of time, and had implored them to pray for him that night. They, American-like, snoozed.

But, what else? Not only was the LORD, the great Yahweh (Jehovah) God satisfied by this macabre sacrifice, but was pleased! Yes. This is what Isaiah reports. He was pleased! "Yet it pleased the LORD to bruise him; he hath put him to grief: when thou shall make his soul an offering for sin..." And why pleased? Because it was by this means that the potential for the salvation of any and all members of the human race, before or after, was achieved. Now a truant and recalcitrant humanity could finally be reconciled to the heart, and very presence of a loving Father. And, like that father in the parable of Luke 15, so this now sprints forward in delight to receive and eternally embrace returning prodigals...

Now, what does that have to do with human suffering? If God, Jesus, or whoever, wishes to go about getting themselves murdered, well enough. But, what does this have to do with us? Everything. We are given the dubious privilege (and, as mentioned above, responsibility) of participating in all this. Did Jesus not counsel us "take up your cross, and follow me (Luke 9:23)?" Did Paul not say, "I am crucified with Christ...(Gal. 2:20)?" Even so, when we willingly accept the providential sufferings that God determines to distribute to each one of us, with an eye toward the cross, we are de facto participants in this great work of eternal redemption. We fulfill the typological association of what the snake-bitten Jewish wanderers did when they looked up to Moses' brass snake in order to be healed.

So, Metallica was right, after all? Well, partly, but not exactly. God uses this suffering (which is always buffered, limited, controlled, and meticulously planned: so he avers) to strengthen, teach, challenge, improve, and sanctify his people. He does not enjoy human suffering the way an Epicurean relishes a delicious, spicy dish. He takes pleasure in it for the cathartic, constructive result in brings about in the character of those exercised thereby. The Jobs, Joni Eareckson Tadas, and Pat Bickles of this world (and the next) would be among the first to assert this very fact.

The formerly sword wielding Peter speaks extensively of this in his first epistle. He learned, as we must, that, as squats are the "king of exercises," so suffering is the king of spiritual disciplines. It gets the results nothing else ever could. Rats.

SEMINALIA

According to Christian theology, Jesus paid for the sins of the human race (provisionally for all men, but according to Calvin, effectually, only for the elect), by dying on the cross. This crunching event covered the chronological space of six hours. He was nailed up by 0900 (am), and dead, and off the cross by 1500 (3:00 pm). If one includes the abuses of the "trial" and scourging he underwent in the hours preceding his crucifixion, the entire ordeal lasted no more than 18 hours or so.

Lucifer, on the other hand, since the moment God "found iniquity in him" (Ezekiel 28:15), and for the last 6,000 years of human history (as reckoned by Biblical chronology), and for the rest of eternity will be suffering for (on account of) the sins of mankind. He is suffering as being held culpable for these sins, having instigated them initially in the Garden of Eden, and previously in heaven on his own. He is also held responsible for the sins of all the fallen angels, now devils, whom he influenced in some mysterious way to defect with himself from the side of God and his glory, to his own purposes and intentions.

What suffering, you may ask? The shame, opprobrium, blame, and punishment for this defection and rebellion has to be staggering. No other creature in the universe enjoyed such an exalted position, and advantages. He was at once the most beautiful, brightest, most musical, and most loved and honored of all God's angels. From this pinnacle of perfection, power, and privilege, he plummeted to the most loathed, cursed, blamed, and hated of all beings. And, prophetically, he is expected to remain, irremediably in this status forever… And, in addition to this, an ocean of infinite torment and agony awaits him, and can by no means be prevented or ameliorated… ever!

So, as the azazel (scapegoat) mentioned above, Lucifer has been "bearing the sins of mankind" for 6,000 years, as compared with Jesus' 6 hours! Now, one must ask here, who is the one doing the heavy lifting?

And why, one may ask, being as brilliant as he is, would he ever do such a thing in the first place? Again, this question is ultimately unanswerable, without recourse to some type of personal interview with the being himself, which is difficult, at best. Conjecture is required, and this is but opinion. However, since we have paid for this ride, we may as well see where it will go, hey? Here are some possibles:

1. Satan did not have a choice. He was created for this end. God not only foresaw this outcome, but caused and intended it from the start. If this answer is true, then our Metal theologians have hit far closer to the mark than anyone might have thought…

2. As suggested earlier in "The Process," perhaps he in some strange way "volunteered" for this job out of an inexplicable love relationship toward his maker (which also would support the whole concept of "symbiosis," since God willingly allowed it).

3. As implied in his dialog with our first mother, Eve, perhaps he felt that God was "holding out" on him, too, and not allowing him to reach his full potential as the tremendously capable creature he was (and still is).

4. Perhaps, as implied in the "I wills" of Isaiah 14, when confronted with the immense, infinite and eternal glory that will ultimately be heaped upon God's son Jesus, he burned with jealousy, believing that he, himself was far more worthy than any mortal human could ever be to receive such blessedness (knowing that eventually, Jesus would become a mortal human).

Lyrics in the hymn, Lord of the Dance, "It's hard to dance with the Devil on your back…"

In the Metallica song, "The Judas Kiss," near the end, the speaker is clearly Satan. He has a monolog of sorts, and included in this is the phrase, "find a piece of me in all, inside you all…" This is something that even the Holy Spirit of God cannot claim. Though all men are created in the image of God, his particular spirit, according to Christian theology, only resides in the "saved, born again, elect, redeemed, saints," etc. In fact, this is thought to be one of the great advantages of becoming a Christian in the first place. So, in a sense, Satan surpasses even God in this respect of personal influence and inhabitation of men in the world at large.

By some accounts, the total number of humans who will be ultimately with God in heaven is pitifully small, compared to the vast number who will "reject the gospel," and go to be with Satan in the end. In addition, one third of all the angels will wind up accompanying him, forever.

Christians risk, at worst, torture and martyrdom (death). Satan's devoted risk temporal death, as well as eternal destruction with their master. Who is risking more to serve his boss?

To cash in on nearly all gospel promises, one must die first. Most of Satan's best stuff is given here in this world, in this life. Satan can make you rich in this world. Jesus usually reserves this for the next. There is a large contingent of Christians who would contest this, but these are also considered heretics by many other believers. These "wealth seeking saints" are called by their detractors: "health-wealth, name it- claim it, or prosperity gospel" advocates.

Who is braver? Jesus, or Satan? Consider these thoughts:

1. Satan's one third of angels must confront twice as many (two-thirds) of their counterparts.

2. Satan can only gather intelligence, and react. God's side already knows, infallibly, what the enemy will do next. Though, apparently Satan does have extensive knowledge of the future, this is still limited.

3. God's power is infinite. What possible fear could his servants have? He, and his enjoy complete "air supremacy," whereas Satan's fighters much ever face greater numbers, firepower, and advantage.

As the redoubtable Mr. Anton LaVey states in his Satanic Bible, the Church (that is, Christianity) could not, could never have either existed in the first place, or "stay in business" now without the original, and now constant input of Lucifer. There would have been no need for Jesus, and he would be unemployed, at least in regard to his role as "Savior."

Who among us has not both eaten, and enjoyed "forbidden fruit?" What would the world be without this sweet, but naughty produce?

In a sense, the very nail scars in the hands of Christ are an eternal tribute to Lucifer's power, craft, and cunning... Jesus could have no claim to the title, "Lamb of God" if it were not for him.

It is a common saying that, "Nothing is ever solved by violence." Yet, in a sense, nothing that is ever solved, is solved without it. In warfare, fights, police arrests, the collection of taxes, parenting, the passing and enforcement of laws, and on and on, either the act or implied threat violence carries the day. And, is God any different? Is not the cross one of the most violent actions ever carried out? To base the entire glory of God (1 Cor. 15), for eternity, on this one bloody event is a bit telling, is it not? And, does not God use incredibly violent threats to enforce his purpose (Rev. 14, Mark 9, etc.)?

The Christians freely admit that, without the inclusion of eternity (or, heaven, if you will), nothing about the gospel makes any sense....

SYMBIOSIS LIVES!